Companion Planting

The Ultimate Guide to Everything You Need to Know for Successful Companion Gardening

Copyright 2015

Table Of Contents

Introduction 1

Chapter 1: Starting with the Basics 2

Chapter 2: Advantages of Companion Planting 5

Chapter 3: Disadvantages of Companion Planting 9

Chapter 4: The Importance of Soil 11

Chapter 5: Designing your Garden 15

Chapter 6: A Brief Guide to Companion Plants 20

Conclusion 24

Introduction

I want to thank you and congratulate you for downloading the book, Companion Planting: *The Ultimate Guide to Everything You Need to Know for Successful Companion Gardening.*

This book contains helpful information about companion planting, what is involved and how you can easily begin.

Companion planting is a smart and enjoyable way to grow more of the vegetables, flowers, and herbs that you love! By combining plants that work well together, you have a much higher chance of growing healthy plants, in larger than normal amounts.

You will soon discover what essential things you must know for a successful garden, along with which plants you can grow.

This book will explain to you tips and techniques that will help you successfully pick plants that work well with each other, and design and create a garden suitable to your needs!

Thanks again for downloading this book, I hope you enjoy it!

Chapter 1:
Starting with the Basics

One of the most satisfying activities anyone can engage in is the art and practice of gardening. Indeed, nothing can compare to the feel of moist, dark soil on one's fingertips or the wonder of watching seeds sprout, bud and grow to fruition. Practically anyone can start their gardening ventures with soil, a couple of basic hand tools and some seeds. However, many novice gardeners often make the mistake of planting too few varieties of plants in a single flower bed.

The notion that each plant has to have its own pot or bed is a misconception that beginners usually hold to. Contrary to that popular belief, plants actually grow better when they are positioned with herbs, ornamentals and fruits that complement them. This chapter will give you a general overview of a method called intercropping, before the next segments introduce you to the advantages and disadvantages of companion planting.

What is companion planting?

Companion planting is the practice of raising different kinds of plants in the same bed or pot to maximize space and potential benefits that the plants can provide for one another. Space maximization is just one of several benefits of companion planting. Other advantages include natural shade provision, pest control, less soil erosion and the facilitation of nitrogen cycles.

When did companion planting start?

No one knows the exact date when companion planting came about, however it is known that this method of intercropping has been used by the Iroquois for as long as they could remember. For the Iroquois, though plants are non-motile creatures, they are still filled with life and thus are sensitive to their immediate surroundings. The Iroquois believe that plants grown together should be harvested and eaten together as they are gifts from God. The plants are also said to be a reminder from their God that communities thrive best when members complement, protect and nurture each other.

Who can engage in companion planting?

Absolutely anyone can try companion planting. This type of gardening is especially ideal for backyard gardens that have limited space. Gardeners who have just started their adventures in soil and plants are also highly encouraged to look into companion planting. If you live in an apartment or you think your backyard is too small to raise a lot of herbs and vegetables, then learning which plants are best suited to grow near each other will help you grow a variety of vegetables and herbs without taking a toll on the available space.

Of course, gardeners who have years of experience, or those who have access to bigger plots of land can also benefit greatly from companion planting. Science has studied the seemingly mysterious aspects of certain plants that enable them to grow together. Numerous experiments have been conducted to answer how and why companion plants tend to have a greater yield than plants that are raised on their own, or simply with the same species. Also, because of the pest control benefit of companion planting, most plants grown using this method are healthier than the average garden plants, making this method ideal for almost all kinds of gardeners.

Chapter 2:
Advantages of Companion Planting

Now that you are familiar with the concept and definition of companion planting, you will want to know what you and your plants can get out of engaging in such a method. The list and explanations below cover the basic benefits that all gardeners who practice companion planting enjoy. Hopefully, after this chapter you will be convinced that the best way to keep your garden healthy and beautiful the natural way is by means of providing your plants with suitable neighbors.

What are the benefits of companion planting?

Companion planting has many benefits, as stated in the prior chapter. This section will tackle those benefits in detail.

1. **Space Maximization**

   The best way to define what space maximization means for gardeners is to give you a vivid example.

   Imagine an average raised bed garden. Let us say that the garden has three beds to start with. If the gardener is not knowledgeable about companion planting, he or she will most probably plant corn in one bed, pole beans in the other and pumpkins in the last bed. It is also unlikely that the gardener will think of making a trellis over the beds, on which fruit-bearing vines can be encouraged to grow.

   On the other hand, a gardener who is familiar with the concept of companion planting will know that corn, pole beans and pumpkins are the legendary "three sisters". In companion planting, the "three sisters" are probably the most common and most successful plant combination. It is also the easiest arrangement of plants to care for, which makes it an ideal starting point for novices.

In the end, the gardener with knowledge about companion planting will be able to save two beds for other plants he or she may want to cultivate. Also, this gardener will probably raise a small lattice over the raised beds where he or she can cultivate vines. Note that this gardener can plant at least three plants in the other two raised beds, making the yield three times greater and with three times the variety than that of the average raised bed garden.

2. Natural Pest Control

Some plants like radishes and dwarf zinnias act as lures for pests. When planted in between or among vegetables that are prone to insect predators, the radishes and dwarf zinnias attract the pests to themselves, thus protecting the other crops. Often, the lured pests also contribute to the health of the plants that attracted them away from their original hosts.

Companion planting uses this logic to keep gardens safe from pests without the use of chemical pesticides. This makes the crops safer to eat, and the absence of chemical pesticides makes for a healthier soil. Aside from distracting pests from delicate vegetables however, companion planting also allows for the luring of beneficial insects. The fragrances and nectars of some flowers and fruits planted alongside vegetables can help in introducing helpful insects to the garden.

3. **Natural Shade**

   This is yet another way for companion plants to help one another. The taller, more mature plants provide a good source of shade and wind protection for the shorter plants. On the other hand, leafy vegetables such as lettuce help to camouflage seedlings from birds and intense sunlight. Their wide leaves also shade the soil, locking in moisture and keeping the bed from drying out.

4. **Less Soil Erosion**

   Some people think that planting a variety of vegetables, herbs and flowers in one bed is detrimental to the soil quality of the garden. This is a common misconception.

   Gardeners who engage in companion planting know their vegetables and herbs very well. They can tell which plants have long, deep penetrating roots and which plants have short, creeping roots. They use this knowledge to make sure that the plants next to each other do not rid the soil of all its nutrients, or compete with each other for essential minerals. In return, the application of this knowledge ensures that all neighbouring plants receive the nutrition and space they need for optimum growth while keeping the soil tightly packed and healthy.

5. **Greater Yield, Healthier Plants**

   The art of companion planting encourages healthier plants, and healthier plants give rise to a bountiful harvest. Scientists and farmers alike have learned that gardens employing the techniques of companion planting have a greater yield than gardens using the monoculture method. These increases in yield and plant health are attributed to the well-planned ecosystem that acts as the basis of companion planting.

Chapter 3:
Disadvantages of Companion Planting

While there are many benefits to be gained from companion planting, it is important to note that like other methods of gardening, intercropping can also be the source of some disadvantages. This chapter is dedicated to exploring those disadvantages to better inform your decision as a gardener. After this chapter, you should have a better grasp on the subject of companion planting and be able to make balanced, informed decisions regarding this method.

1. **Fussy Plants**

   Like people and animals, plants can be picky when it comes to their neighbours. Some plants just do not sit well with others and this can cause nutrient imbalances, or in worse cases, wilting and the eventual death of an ill placed plant. For years, scientists and farmers learned about which plants grow well with each other by trial and error. Though there are modern methods to determine which plants are destined to be best friends, the issue of highly sensitive vegetation still remains a problem for companion planting.

2. **Research, Research, Research**

   This is probably the biggest disadvantage when it comes to companion planting. To avoid multiple crop losses due to poor planning and inadequate knowledge, gardeners using the companion planting method must always be up to date with their research involving vegetables, herbs and fruits. Companion planting demands rigorous planning before, during and after the planting process. This can prove to be too tedious to gardeners who are used to the monoculture type of gardening where specific crops are planted in their respective beds.

3. Competition for Water and Nutrients

What happens when a gardener does not do his or her research regarding which plants are good companions for each other? Well, to make it clear- disaster strikes.

While well-planned gardens can utilize companion planting efficiently, poorly planned gardens will inevitably subject plants to competition for water and essential nutrients. This will also rid the soil of its minerals quicker, thus making the soil quality deteriorate. In the end, having to compete for water and other nutrients may decrease the vigour of crops, and instead of having a garden with increased yield, the gardener may find him or herself with less crops.

These disadvantages are all rooted to poor planning and an inadequate understanding of plant life, cycles and the importance of a balanced ecosystem. If you are more than willing to spend time learning about which plants are most likely to thrive with companions, then it is less probable that you will experience any of these drawbacks.

Chapter 4:
The Importance of Soil

Now that you know the advantages and disadvantages of companion planting, you will need to know the essentials of a well-planned garden. The first and foremost requirement of any good garden is soil. High quality soil means more nutrients and minerals for your crops, which in turn means healthier, bigger plants for your garden.

Like all organic gardening methods, companion planting lays an emphasis on the quality of a garden's soil. Some gardeners like to purchase compost soil from nearby garden centers while others prefer making their own.

This chapter will introduce you to the benefits and necessity of having high quality soil in your garden before you think about introducing seeds and seedlings. There will also be a step by step guide included here to help you create a compost pit of your own.

The Three Types of Soil

Gardeners can tell if the soil in their plots is sandy by doing the *ball test*. This is a simple test to determine the density of your soil and if it will be good enough for flowers, herbs and vegetables. To perform the ball test, simply scoop some soil from your backyard or proposed garden plot and then quickly roll the soil in between your palms. The results will tell you what kind of soil you have, and whether or not it needs more attention and organic matter before you introduce plants.

1. **Sandy Soil**

   If you perform the ball test and the soil in your hands crumbles immediately or refuses to hold a spherical shape, then you most probably have sandy soil. This type of soil holds very little water, if any at all. This means that you will constantly have to monitor the moisture levels of your plots to avoid them from drying out. This kind of soil also has less nutrients compared to loamy and clay soil. To remedy this, gardeners advise fattening the soil with organic matter first before planting in it.

2. **Clay Soil**

   This kind of soil, when subjected to the ball test, produces a tight, sticky clump that is capable of holding its shape for a considerable amount of time. It is denser than sandy and loamy soil. Clay soil is darker than sandy soil, but lighter when compared to loamy soil. This type of soil easily becomes water logged and can make your plots prone to flooding. It also lacks enough airspace for your plants and seeds to breathe underground, thus you may have to keep moving the soil for better aeration and mineral distribution.

3. **Loamy Soil**

   This is by far the best kind of soil to plant flowers, herbs and vegetables in. You will know if your plot has loamy soil if, after performing the ball test, you end up with a well-formed soil ball, that loses its shape after some time. This means that the soil is neither too dense nor too loose. It provides the perfect environment for growing plants because it does not get water-logged and it is considered to be mineral-rich.

Composting: The Solution to Soil Problems

So what do you do if your plot has sandy or clay soil? The best organic solution that you can immediately set into action is creating your own compost pit. A compost pit is the place where you store soil and decaying organic matter. Materials like fruit peels, dead leaves, vegetable left-overs, paper and animal droppings make good fertilizers for the soil. Composting speeds up the time needed for the complete decay of these materials until their nutrients are integrated with the soil.

Composting is also a good way to make use of biodegradable waste you may have sitting in your trash bins. Not only will you be helping your garden, you will also be contributing to a better environment.

Creating a Compost Pit

The first step to creating a compost is to gather as much biodegradable materials as you can. Biodegradable materials include fruit skins, kitchen scraps, dried leaves and even wood chips or paper. You can also include meat and dairy products; however it will be better to use those in a compost pit that are not within your house's premises.

Once you have at least 30cm or 1ft deep worth of biodegradable materials, you can start constructing a compost box or container. You can also opt to buy such a container or simply recycle an old water drum. If you are sure about where you want to use the compost, you can also choose to dig directly in your garden and mix your compost materials in the ground itself.

After deciding on what kind of container you want to use for your compost, you can begin layering the materials. Start with a layer of soil. For those who choose not to use any container at all and have dug into the ground, you can skip this step. Next, pour in a few inches of compost material. Finding the right balance for a compost mix takes time and experience, though you should not worry about failing so long as you make it a point to alternate the layers of biodegradable materials and soil.

Continue to layer the materials and soil until the container is filled, or until the hole in the ground is level again with the rest of the garden. Cover your compost pit. If you just dug a hole in the ground, you can use tough cloth stretched over the hole or a thick sheet of tarpaulin as a cover.

Leave the compost for a few weeks. You can check on the mix from time to time. Some gardeners even stir the soil and materials every other week just to improve air circulation. Your finished compost pit should not smell of rot. In fact, the best compost pits produce dark, moist and slightly crumbly soil that is sweet-smelling. Once you think your compost is ready, you can use it in your plots, pots or garden beds.

Chapter 5:
Designing your Garden

The next step to creating a successful garden using companion planting methods is to plan in detail, where and how big your plots will be. You need to pay attention to this step of the process because like what was explained in the previous chapters, most disadvantages of companion planting come about when the garden is poorly planned. This chapter will focus on the layout of your garden, and how you can maximize your space with raised beds and other ideas for plant containers.

The Layout

If you have very limited space, you might want to check out books on square foot gardening or wall gardening. These garden layouts will provide you with ideas on how to make the most out of your space without sacrificing aesthetics and quality.

For companion planting to work, you must know which beds will be placed near each other, and whether or not you want to have a mixture of herbs and flowers in your garden as well. You can choose to have a garden concentrated on raising vegetables only, but remember that having flowers, herbs and fruit-bearing plants are also beneficial for companion planting. There are some insects that only flowers attract, and some pests that only certain herbs repel. Below are a few steps on how to get started with the layout of your garden.

1. **Consult an Expert**

   If you are new to the gardening experience, some tips from plant experts and garden veterans may be in order. You do not necessarily need to consult a landscape designer for your garden plan, especially if budget is a concern. You can choose to visit a garden centre and ask for their advice on what beds suit your space best. You can also go around your neighbourhood and make friends with fellow gardeners. At this stage of your gardening career, it is important to create a network of people who know what they are doing and who will be willing to help you.

   Talk to your friends or the experts you find and ask them about round beds, raised beds, trellises, fences and wall gardens. Do not hesitate to ask for their recommendation when it comes to designing your garden. However, bear in mind that their ideas should support and not overrule whatever your choice may be.

2. **Draw your Plans**

   Lay a sheet of white paper on a table top or stick it to a wall. Take out your pencils and erasers and create a rough guide for what you want your garden to look like. Your sketch does not need to be perfect; however a detailed draft is better than a very general one.

   Remember to take note of the measurements of your yard or extra space, and take that into consideration when you draft your garden plans. After you are done with the first draft, consult with your friends at the garden centre, or experts again. Listen well to the advice they have to give you and take their ideas into consideration.

3. **Check the area of your proposed plant beds**

   Before you execute your plans, ask yourself these questions to know whether or not your garden design is feasible and practical:

   a. Is the water easily accessible?

   b. Is it in reach of ample sunlight?

   c. Is there enough shade?

   d. Is it safe from kids and pets?

   e. Is it shielded from strong wind?

   f. Is the area safe from floods?

   If all your answers to these questions are resounding affirmatives, then you are ready to begin fixing your garden area.

4. **Create your first set of plant beds**

   Whether you choose a raised bed or an in-ground bed is completely up to you. However, most gardeners who use companion planting techniques also subscribe to raised-bed gardens. Regardless of what plant bed you decide on creating, remember to design it in such a way that there is ample space between the beds and that there is also a delineated pathway where you can step. The pathway will help you further reduce erosion, and will also keep your garden beds easier to clean and maintain.

5. Maintain a tool shed

After clearing the area and successfully creating your garden beds, you should invest time and effort in making a tool shed. The tool shed will serve as your go-to place for both seeds and tools. It should be easily accessible from your garden and should be well protected. Your tool shed need not be expensive or intricately designed. Focus on creating a functional tool shed that will hold all of your gardening materials and tools.

6. Invest in a crop or plant nursery

You may want to have a nursery for your seedlings after you have gained considerable experience in gardening. The nursery will serve as the first home of young plants that will be transplanted to the bigger garden plots before they reach maturity. Having a nursery is useful for gardeners who want to cultivate herbs and sensitive plants.

7. Consider fences for your garden plots

This step is optional. If there are no children or untrained pets in your house, then you can choose not to put fences around your garden plots. However, if you fear that your plants will be trampled on by paws or little feet, it is a good idea to have the foresight to install sturdy fences. Like the shed, fences do not need to be expensive. In fact, you can create your fences with whittled branches or wood that you can find along roads, or forest paths.

Fences and trellises are very useful in companion planting as they provide more space on which vines and other creepers can grow on.

8. Walls and Recycled Containers

As a last effort to maximize your space, you can look into how wall gardens are created and maintained. Remember that companion planting also works with plant boxes, and long recycled containers. So long as you have enough space for the companion plants to grow, enough soil for them to gather nutrients from and adequate planning, your wall and recycled container gardens will be successful as well.

Be creative when it comes to plant beds and containers. You can use soft drink bottles for hanging aerial plants or old tires to create instant round beds. You can also use the same tires as storage for your compost.

Chapter 6:
A Brief Guide to Companion Plants

At last, you are ready to learn all about the different plant combinations that make companion planting a fruitful endeavor. This chapter will focus on which plants make good growth buddies, which plants attract and repel insects or pests and which plants do not play well with each other. Once you master which plants should be planted together and which plants would do best to avoid each other, you will have an easier time planning and designing your garden.

The Three Sisters

This is the most common, easiest combination of all the plant combinations. As explained in the second chapter, the three sisters' combination is composed of beans, pumpkins and corn. The corn provides shade for the pumpkins; the beans support the much needed nitrogen cycle, and the pumpkins cover the soil with their leaves, keeping the bed moist. Pumpkins also have prickly leaves that deter pets and the random raccoon from invading the bed.

Onions, leeks and chives

This group of plants grow best with carrots and tomatoes. The onions and their relatives are a good natural repellent for aphids, flies and some spiders. They protect the tomatoes from pests and other bad insects.

Onions can also be used as a companion plant for roses. As strange as it sounds, the tandem of onions and roses are one of the easiest to grow in the average backyard garden. The onions protect the roses from aphids and mildew, while the roses draw nectar-loving pollinators to rest of the garden bed.

Corn and tomatoes

These two plants are among the best of friends. Aside from being beneficial to each other's growth, they also have a common worm enemy. They can also be planted alongside beans, pumpkins, peas and potatoes. Surround the tomatoes and corn with basil for protection from aphids and pests, and you'll have a garden plot of soup vegetables helping and protecting each other. Peas provide extra doses of nitrogen in the soil for corn plants that demand much of this element during the peak of their growth.

You can also add soybeans or snap beans to the plot if you happen to have a lot of corn. Remember that corn is among the hungriest plants, and it is known to drain the soil of essential nutrients. Having soybeans or snap beans in the same plot means that it is less likely for the garden bed to run out of nitrogen; in addition soy beans act as a repellent for certain bugs and beetles.

Chervil and chives

These plants are used to enhance the growth and flavor of carrots and radishes. If you add rosemary and sage to the same plot, you will be able to effectively repel carrot flies among other pests.

Carrots do not grow well in the presence of dill. The dill hampers the carrots' growth, and thus counters the effects of the rosemary, sage and chives.

Fennel

Unfortunately, fennel is not suitable as a companion plant since many herbs and vegetables have been proven to be stunted by its presence. If you want to grow fennel in your garden, you can do so in small pots where they will not get in the way of other plants.

Marigolds and Roses

These pretty flowers are good companions for tomatoes, strawberries and beans. They effectively encourage the growth of their fellow garden bed plants and aid in deterring harmful nematodes from populating the soil. They also provide a splash of color to any garden plot, and are thus attractive to pollinators.

Cucumber and Corn

In a garden bed where cucumber and corn grow together, you can expect a very high crop yield come harvest time. Cucumber also helps the growth of beans, peas, radishes and sunflowers. Because of their vines, cucumbers help stabilizing the tall corn and provide shade for the smaller peas and radishes.

Oregano and Broccoli

Oregano is a natural repellent of the infamous cabbage fly. In addition, it helps maintain the tightness of the soil as its roots stabilize the top layers while the broccoli's roots anchor the middle layers.

Stinging Nettle

Though science has yet to explain this garden mystery, vegetables that are grown in the presence of stinging nettle show unrivalled vigor and crop yield. This kind of nettle also helps in keeping weeds at bay, and thus contributes to soil health.

Cabbage and Cauliflower

Although these two vegetables are closely related, they do not grow well together. Recent studies have shown that they compete for the same minerals and nutrients, and thus tend to tire the soil. The result is a poor yield, if any at all.

The examples of companion plants in this chapter are only a few of the common garden vegetables and flowers that can and should be planted together. There are only a few exceptions to companion planting such as fennel. If you take the time to study which plants grow well in the presence of other plants, then you will be able to come up with a list of your own that will help you and other gardeners in the future.

Conclusion

Thank you again for downloading this book!

I hope this book was able to help you learn more about companion planting.

The next step is to put this information to use, and begin growing your garden!

Remember to take your time, and start slow. Plan your garden thoroughly and make sure it's suitable for the plants you wish to grow. Select the plants you want, and begin your journey with companion planting!

Also, don't forget to claim your FREE bonus e-book on how to grow tomatoes!
Download your copy HERE or click the link below:

http://bit.ly/1ODGQbJ

Finally, if you enjoyed this book, please take the time to share your thoughts and post a review on Amazon. It'd be greatly appreciated!

Thank you and good luck!

www.ingramcontent.com/pod-product-compliance
Lightning Source LLC
LaVergne TN
LVHW021750060526
838200LV00052B/3558